Contents

When 'him' is used in the text, it refers to both male and female
adolescents. When it refers specifically to the male, it is described as
the 'boy' or the 'male adolescent'; when it refers specifically to the
female, it is described as the 'girl' or the 'female adolescent'.

Acknowledgements

A number of people have been especially helpful during the preparation of this book, and I wish to acknowledge and thank them for this. My thanks to Anna Freud for her continued help and critical comments; to the staff of the Brent Consultation Centre and the Centre for the Study of Adolescence for help in clarifying some of the ideas presented; to Jonathan Croall of Penguin Education and Alison Wertheimer of MIND (National Association for Mental Health) for their many suggestions and careful editing.

I am especially grateful to my wife, Eglé. The ideas and formulations were discussed with her throughout the preparation of this book.

Pelican Books
Mind Specials

**Adolescent Disturbance
and Breakdown**

Moses Laufer

Moses Laufer was born in Montreal; he is now settled in
London. He is the Director of the Brent Consultation Centre
and the Centre for the Study of Adolescence. He is a
psychoanalyst qualified for work with adults and children;
for a number of years he has been on the part-time staff of
the Hampstead Child Therapy Clinic. He is a Member of
the British Psychoanalytical Society. His publications on
adolescence have appeared in various professional journals;
he has also lectured extensively in Europe, U S A and Canada.

MIND (National Association for Mental Health) is a charity
concerned with the needs of the mentally ill and handicapped,
and with the promotion of mental health. It draws attention
to inadequacies in the health service and campaigns for better
standards of care. It runs homes, schools and hostels as well
as advisory services, courses, conferences and a public
information department. It has over one hundred active local
groups who are concerned with alleviating mental stress in the
community.

MIND, 22 Harley Street, London W1N 2ED. Tel: 01 637 0741.

MOSES LAUFER

Penguin Books
in association with MIND

ADOLESCENT DISTURBANCE AND BREAKDOWN

Penguin Books Ltd,
Harmondsworth, Middlesex, England
Penguin Books Inc, 7110 Ambassador Road,
Baltimore, Md 21207, U.S.A.
Penguin Books Australia Ltd,
Ringwood, Victoria, Australia
Penguin Books Canada Ltd,
41 Steelcase Road West,
Markham, Ontario, Canada
Penguin Books (N.Z.) Ltd,
182—190 Wairau Road, Auckland 10, New Zealand

First published 1975
Copyright © Moses Laufer, 1974

Made and printed in Great Britain by
Compton Printing Ltd, Aylesbury

Set in IBM Univers

CHAPTER 1
INTRODUCTION

It is increasingly being recognized that the incidence of mental disturbance and illness in the community is more widespread than had been thought. It is also being acknowledged that a great deal more can be done about prevention, treatment and care. This is especially true of the adolescent, who until recently was often dismissed as somebody who was 'going through adolescence' rather than being recognized as a person with emotions, problems, anxieties and ideals.

This book describes the psychological development of the adolescent, and discusses illness and breakdown which occur during this period. It gives a view of the part played by adolescence in a person's mental development, and indicates some of the signs which tell us that the adolescent is vulnerable to disturbance or mental illness, or to the possibility of what is commonly described as 'breakdown'.

The period of adolescence, that is, the years from about thirteen to twenty-one, is often referred to as the 'gap' which exists between childhood and adulthood. Work with normal adolescents and treatment of mentally disturbed adolescents and adults, however, has shown us that this period has a major part to play in the person's development to emotional maturity. Our increased knowledge about normal development and about mental disturbance and illness makes us less inclined to expect that the adolescent who is showing signs of stress will 'grow out of it' or will be able to 'pull himself together'. Prevention of mental disturbance or illness in adolescence or adulthood is now of greater concern to many people, including the parent, the teacher, the family doctor, the social worker and the police officer. A person does not have to have actually broken down or be obviously mentally ill before something must be done to help.

Prevention of mental disturbance or illness safeguards the adolescent's progress to normal adulthood, but this is only one of the important concerns we have; prejudices and misconceptions about mental illness often make it difficult for those concerned to understand and accept that an adolescent may be mentally ill or in immediate need of care and help. Many young people, as well as the parents and professional people who work with them, may react initially by denying that a problem exists; they may try to explain away the problem in ways which help to dismiss its severity. The isolated adolescent may simply be thought of as shy; the very depressed adolescent may be considered lazy; the adolescent who has attempted suicide may be thought of as attention-seeking. Others may try to explain the problem in ways which imply blame, whether that blame is directed at the parents, at society, or at some recognizable force. Such explanations, however valid they sometimes seem to be, disregard the fact that once the person has reached adolescence the mental disturbance or the illness which is present exists inside the person himself, irrespective of its origins. It also means that unless something is done to help, he may continue to live with his disturbance or illness, no matter what changes take place in his living circumstances, his education or in his work.

Those who are concerned professionally with helping or treating the adolescent must recognize the fact that the person who is mentally disturbed or ill or vulnerable to breakdown needs help for himself, independently of help offered to his parents or to anyone else involved. Some people, instead of recognizing the extent of disturbance, will try to help by giving advice, by being kind and friendly, by reassuring the person that he will be all right, by prescribing something which temporarily removes the symptoms of the trouble, or by promising that one sort of help or another will be the answer to his problems. Such approaches disregard the fact that adolescence may be a 'second chance' for many young people, and that it is a second chance which can be dependent on appropriate assessment and careful help or treatment. (This is discussed in more detail on pp. 56–63 and 68–69.)

Assessment, help or treatment must begin with a detailed knowledge of the normal psychological development of the adolescent. We can then differentiate between those who are developing normally and those who are mentally disturbed, ill or vulnerable to breakdown. We can also gauge more carefully how effective are our efforts to help. Beyond this, we can begin to ask whether our services reflect the needs of the mentally disturbed, ill or vulnerable adolescent, or whether we are still tied to traditional, and sometimes not very effective, ways of helping.

CHAPTER 2
MENTAL DEVELOPMENT IN ADOLESCENCE

This chapter will concentrate mainly on a description of the mental changes which normally take place in adolescence, and the ways in which these changes affect the behaviour of the adolescent.

The period of adolescence lasts from seven to nine years in a person's life: as a time of mental development, it covers the years from about twelve or thirteen to twenty or twenty-one. It begins, in psychological terms, at the time that physical sexual maturity starts to take place; this can vary quite normally from between the ages of twelve or thirteen to fifteen or sixteen. Although the end of adolescence cannot be described with the same certainty as the start, it is considered to have ended, in terms of mental development, when the person's sexual identity has been established and when his ways of dealing with stress or anxiety have been fixed. This usually occurs at about the age of twenty or twenty-one.

Physical sexual maturity constitutes a major change in the life of every person: a boy can now produce semen, impregnate a female and father a child; a girl begins to menstruate and (usually soon after her first menstruation has occurred) is able to bear a child. The psychological reactions to the physical ability to be a father or mother are a major part of what adolescence is about, but the way in which each person responds mentally to this is determined, to a very great extent, by the person's history up to the time of physical maturity.

What are the mental adjustments which have to take place so that the adolescent can feel free to leave behind his childhood dependency on his parents and to begin to function more as an independent person? Why is it that some adolescents find it difficult or impossible to allow these changes to take place? It is common to try to explain an adolescent's behaviour in terms of the external demands being made on him by school, work, friends or parents. These explanations contain some truth, but they avoid the fact that it is the adolescent's reactions to these demands which are important, and these are determined mainly by his own mental makeup: his conscience, his ideals, his feelings about himself and his fears.

The period of adolescence is often a lonely one. The adolescent often feels a failure because he believes that he has not matched up to a personal ideal; his successes are often felt by him to be only temporary; he may experience guilt and worry because he believes that what he thinks or does is not quite normal, or that he has transgressed against what he considers acceptable, or because he still prefers to remain a child. Some feel not only lonely, but confused and isolated, uncertain as to whether they need be worried about their behaviour or their thoughts.

Stress by itself is not necessarily a sign that something is going wrong; the adolescent whose mental development is progressing normally will also experience stress and doubt. There are many reasons for this: the sexual feelings which come from his own body may create temporary guilt or shame; shyness with the opposite sex may make him feel that he is weak or still a child; inability or hesitation to participate in physical activities such as sports or dancing may create feelings of fear and despondency; masturbation, and the thoughts which often accompany this, can create fears of abnormality; lack of friends can make him feel that he is not liked in comparison with others of his own age.

It is important to know how the adolescent is responding to the stress and to try to establish whether it is interfering with his ability or wish to progress, in terms of his mental development, to adulthood. We can then judge with greater clarity whether there is reason to be concerned about his present and future mental health, but our ability to know when to be concerned depends on a detailed understanding of normal development during this period.

Changes in mental functioning during adolescence

The variations of behaviour during adolescence are so numerous that it is often difficult to decide what is due to temporary stress, and what has to be viewed as a sign of the presence of or vulnerability to more serious mental disturbance. (See Anna Freud, *Psychoanalytic Study of the Child,* 1960.) A closer view of the areas of mental functioning where changes must take place if the person is to be able to move towards adulthood, can help in understanding the meaning of stress to the adolescent. By examining these areas of change and using them as points of reference, we can isolate some common factors from the whole multitude of stresses which exist for every adolescent. This makes it possible for the professional person, parent or the young person himself to understand better the implication of his behaviour.

These areas where changes must take place are as follows:

Relationship with parents

He must move from dependence on his parents towards emotional independence. There should be signs that the adolescent is able to feel that his thoughts and feelings are his own, and not necessarily dependent on how his parents might react. The adolescent will normally be able to risk invoking disapproval from the parents without necessarily feeling that he must give in to them.

Relationship with contemporaries

He should be able to choose as friends other adolescents whose demands and expectations of themselves are no longer the demands of childhood, but are such that they enhance the adolescent's efforts and wishes to become an adult.

Attitude to his body

He should no longer see himself as a child in the care of his parents, but as somebody who feels that his sexually maturing body belongs to him and that he alone is responsible for it. This means that he should feel he is in control of his body, and should be free to use it in a way which he feels to be right.

There are many reasons why even the normal and well-functioning adolescent will have doubts, be unhappy, feel that he is failing, and question whether all is going right with him. During the adolescent period, mood swings will be common and behaviour will be unpredictable. Various forms of experimenting will take place whether they are with people, drugs, jobs or even with himself. Friendships, the questioning of parents' ideals and standards, doubting the adult world, being uncertain about the future, feeling sexually and socially unsure, being in love, or feeling guilty or shameful about private thoughts and actions all contribute to this state.

Most adolescents find appropriate ways of dealing with these inner pressures, and for most of them this period of their lives contributes something of great importance to their future mental health and social functioning. For them, adolescence is a time when uncertainties, new feelings, new anxieties, a new view of themselves, and a new view of others are experienced as part of the pressure to move towards adulthood and as part of giving up the safety and dependence of childhood.

There are other adolescents who respond differently, who feel that this period of their lives is little more than a constant reminder or a confirmation that there is something wrong with them. It is as if unconsciously they know that they are stuck at a particular point in their mental development. The reasons for this may vary enormously; although some are elaborated in Chapters 3 and 4, it can be pointed out here that 'being stuck' can sometimes help to explain a large variety of worrying behaviour usually associated with this age. Some adolescents feel constantly exposed to regressive behaviour, to being pulled back to types of relationships and modes of satisfaction more suited to childhood. This can be seen in the adolescent who needs to spend all his time with his parents because they make him feel wanted, loved and protected; or in the adolescent who needs to be taken care of and fed, and who insists on being treated as the child who is admired and told what to do or not to do; or in the adolescent who insists that his mother or father takes care of his body. For them, help such as advice or counselling is experienced temporarily as a reassurance that they will grow out of it, but they then feel that they have not been understood and that they are as vulnerable as ever.

The psychological changes which I described earlier present every young person with many hurdles, and often make life difficult for those around him. For example, he normally finds that changing the relationship with his parents means giving up his childhood attachments, seeking new forms of satisfaction and new kinds of relationships. At such a time he will temporarily feel that he has 'lost' his parents. Before he is able to replace them with new relationships with contemporaries, he will feel alone and will experience transitory feelings of depression. At the same time he must also feel free to fight his parents, that is, to differ, to argue and to criticize. Although this battle goes on during most of his adolescence, he should eventually reach a point where emotionally he is able to feel on more equal terms with them.

This period is usually a strenuous time for the parents; they may feel that their teenage son or daughter is different from the child they remember. The parents are in a very difficult but important position — on the one hand, the 'adolescent rebellion' is unpleasant, it affects them and they react to this; on the other hand, the adolescent needs them to rebel against, and to make him realize that his conflict is really going on within himself. Familial support can be of great help to the growing adolescent.

If the parents give in too easily to every demand, become depressed by every criticism levelled at them, or try desperately to please the adolescent by always joining in with him and his friends, he may feel that he has harmed or 'destroyed' his parents or that he may be able to do so. He will become frightened by his own power and may find it much more difficult to become a mature adult. Such a sign of 'being stuck' can be observed most clearly in the depressed person who feels worried about what he may have done to his parents, and who reacts to a parent's temporary physical illness with self-accusation and guilt — as if he is responsible in some way. Often, too, such extreme events as death or mental illness of a parent can, for someone who feels that he has not been a good child, act as a confirmation of his feeling that he can harm people; the guilt and the self-accusation which he now feels make it much more difficult for him to become psychologically independent of them.

Stages in development during adolescence

These fundamental changes which should take place as part of normal mental development in adolescence are only to be viewed as a guide. We should not expect to see change from day to day. The process of change is an extended one which takes place over the whole period of adolescence. When considering the appropriateness or inappropriateness of the behaviour or reaction of the adolescent, it is useful and important to remember that the adolescent of thirteen or fourteen is, psychologically, quite different from the adolescent of nineteen or twenty. In other words, some behaviour at thirteen or fourteen may be appropriate and a sign of normal development, whereas the same behaviour at nineteen or twenty may be inappropriate and a sign of the presence of or vulnerability to mental disturbance or illness.

I can illustrate what I mean with some questions. When is it appropriate for an adolescent to want to move away from home? Or, when is it appropriate for him to want to keep things to himself and to exclude his parents from his private behaviour and personal relationships? When is a homosexual relationship a sign of the presence of mental disturbance? When is sexual intercourse premature, that is, when may it be a sign of the presence of anxiety about his normality, and when is it appropriate as part of a relationship with another person? When is friendlessness a sign that he is experiencing mental stress which needs to be viewed seriously? When is the concern about his body — its size, its functioning, its development, its health, its strength — appropriate and when is it a sign of the presence of overconcern? This list of questions can be extended to cover every area of the adolescent's behaviour and functioning, but the important question would still be: when are certain forms of behaviour, reactions, or relationships appropriate and a sign of normal development, and when are they inappropriate and a sign of the presence of or vulnerability to mental disturbance or illness?

A helpful way of answering some of these questions is to consider the normal stresses and the most important preoccupations which exist at different stages in the

adolescent's mental development. Blos (*On Adolescence*, 1962) has divided the period of adolescence into three stages of development — early, middle and late — and he has shown that each stage has certain special 'priorities' of its own.

It is necessary to view psychological development as a continuum, with each period of development playing an important part in determining the way in which subsequent development takes place; in adolescence, each solution to a mental task affects the way in which the rest of the period is experienced. The analogy with physical development can illustrate the point. If a child breaks his leg, and the leg is not properly set, the bone may still heal but the child will limp. This in turn may affect his ability to play sports, to have friends, and to do what other people do. If the broken leg had been set correctly, the result would have been different.

In mental development, including both childhood and adolescence, we can find similar examples. The child who stutters, is shy or frightened, or feels that he is different from other children, is more likely to avoid his peers in adolescence and to stay away from situations where he is compared with them. He will be more inclined to isolate himself so that he does not have to go on experiencing the painful fact that he cannot get on as easily as others. This may force him towards more childish forms of behaviour which in turn stand in the way of more appropriate experiences with friends and contemporaries. By the age of eighteen or nineteen, he may still feel shy and worried about himself, but by this time his view of himself as being different and perhaps abnormal is much more fixed. He may be much more isolated and he may have missed the opportunities for further mental development provided by normal social relationships with contemporaries.

The stages of adolescent development described below are somewhat arbitrary, but they enable us to understand more clearly what is taking place in the mind or, seen from a preventive point of view, what it is that is not taking place. The 'priorities' or preoccupations in the mind of the adolescent fall roughly into three periods:

From twelve or thirteen to fifteen

The main concerns are related to the beginning adjustment to
his physically maturing body; the fight against signs of loss of
self-control related to his newly acquired physical strength and
sexual feelings; against loneliness, isolation and depression; and
against the wish to remain a child and to be cared for by his
parents.

From about fifteen to seventeen or eighteen

The main stresses revolve around the adolescent's efforts to
become emotionally independent of the parents. He begins to
feel that thoughts, wishes and actions are no longer
determined by the expectations of his parents. Contemporaries
now become more important in deciding what is acceptable or
unacceptable. During this time the adolescent is taken up with
the development of his or her body — whether there are any
signs of abnormality, how it compares with the bodies of other
adolescents.

Masturbation for the boy plays an important part in the
effort to try out (in thought) his physically mature body; for
the girl masturbation may sometimes play a part, but this is
not necessarily an important activity. Her experimentations
will be related more to the use of her whole body shown by an
interest in her physical appearance.

From about eighteen to twenty-one

The adolescent begins to view himself or herself as a 'man' or a
'woman'. Social and sexual relationships take on greater
permanence; sexual intercourse is psychologically more
appropriate during these years because the adolescent is now
more prepared to integrate a sexual relationship as part of his
life more easily and more constructively than in the earlier
years. There is a greater acceptance of his sexually mature
body; his sexual identity is now much more fixed.

These are years when the adolescent may feel it to be a
time of crisis in his life, when thoughts and feelings are much

less fluid than previously, and when there is the beginning of a more defined picture of a person whose actions and behaviour are more predictable.

The adolescent's relationship with his parents continues to reflect his independence, but there are also signs of a new kind of relationship with them; he is now more able to feel that he is a person separate from his parents, responsible for his actions, and with a social and sexual life which does not arouse feelings of guilt or shame for being an adult.

Variations in normality during adolescence

A number of things have been left out in the description of priorities or preoccupations which exist during adolescence. To discuss a wide range of adolescent behaviour would lead to the question of the differences between temporary stress and mental disturbance or illness; this will be dealt with in Chapter 4. I have in mind such things as delinquency, lying, failure at school or work, deliberate isolation, promiscuity, friendlessness, early sexual experience, homosexual relationships, drug-taking, and so on. Although it is not wise to dismiss lightly any extreme or uncharacteristic behaviour of an adolescent as simply being part of normal development, one should also guard against constant criticism or concern if he behaves in a way not approved of by the adult world.

These variations in normality during adolescence result from a range of experiences and relationships which include cultural and social variations, the personal characteristics of the parents, family expectations, and the unique experiences which each individual faces as part of normal development. Each sub-culture, religious group, social class, or family unit will have its own expectations of its members, and will contribute basically to the individual's values, expectations and demands of himself. One sub-culture, religion or family may place great importance on honesty, righteousness, or unquestioning respect of and submission to parents; another sub-culture or family may accept delinquency, or may believe that people who look or behave differently from the group are potentially dangerous. Such descriptions of a wide range of behaviour should not be regarded as an account of what constitutes psychological health. When I refer to psychological health in adolescence (or, more generally, to psychological functioning) I refer to an 'inner state' and not primarily to what can be observed. During adolescence the person's inner state is constantly under stress, and this in turn is reflected in his behaviour and reactions.

Although the person's inner state determines the manner in which he responds to demands or expectations of his own or those from other people, there are a number of other factors which normally contribute to stress. The outside world begins to see the person as more responsible for his own behaviour and, combined with this, friends begin to demand a level and form of behaviour which is different from that which existed in childhood. The earlier attitudes of society to the child and to those forms of behaviour which were once accepted by other children are now no longer acceptable. The world no longer revolves around the family and the parents, but begins to take into account a much broader field of rights and wrongs.

It is common for the adolescent to deny any link with his own childhood, and he may therefore try to reject any signs of childish behaviour (even though at the same time he may participate in it with his friends). The conflict within himself, especially during the early period, revolves around not giving in to his wish to enjoy childish satisfactions, but to 'try out' new ways of dealing with stress. The young adolescent feels he must make the effort to become independent by going to dances, by having nothing to do with his parents, or by suddenly adopting behaviour which is uncharacteristic of him. As the adolescent nears adulthood, he is at one and the same time taken up with the question of his psychological development and with the way he is functioning in the outside world. He is expected, for example, to know somewhat more definitely what occupation he will choose or what profession he may follow. Perhaps, more painfully, he is expected to know what his own personal limitations are. On the other hand, it is not at all uncommon for him to have great difficulty and to feel guilty in acknowledging the fact that he may be better equipped than some of his friends, brothers or sisters, or even his parents. Whether the adolescent can accept his own limitations or strengths will depend primarily on the manner in which his earlier relationships within the family have helped or hindered him; that is, the ways in which these relationships and experiences have determined the kind of 'inner state' which exists when the person reaches adolescence.

Childhood and adolescence

What is the relationship between childhood and adolescence? Freud began, in the early 1900s, the revolution in the understanding of mental disturbance and illness. Following Freud, who described in intricate detail the factors in the person's development which act as the foundation for his whole psychological life, his daughter, Anna Freud *(Normality and Pathology in Childhood,* 1965), and others have studied and written about the normal and the abnormal mental development of the child. From this we can understand with much greater precision the meaning of certain forms of behaviour in children and adolescents, and we can also be much more certain about some of the danger signs which may be present in the child's and the adolescent's development.

We begin by assuming that behaviour and development are not accidental. We may find ourselves unable to explain the meaning of certain forms of behaviour, but we nevertheless assume that a person's behaviour and development are reflections of his history, including what has gone on in his own mind and what has happened between him and his parents, guardians or anyone *in loco parentis*. Constitutional factors are also important, but we do not know how to gauge their relative effect on psychological development.

Up to about the age of five, the child's behaviour is governed by what he thinks will be approved or disapproved of by his parents. It is as if the parents represent law and morality, and the child feels obliged to respect this in order to be loved. A very important step in mental development takes place at the age of about five and it is only then that we can talk of a child's 'conscience' or 'ideals'. It is at about this time that the wishes and the demands of the parents become part of the child's own mental makeup. Freud (*New Introductory Lectures on Psychoanalysis*, 1933) referred to this as the 'superego', a part of the mind which now makes its own demands, has its own expectations and its own criteria for approval or disapproval. This means that, whether or not the parents are present, the child begins to judge himself, approve of his own behaviour, have feelings of self-regard, and experience feelings of guilt and shame if he has done something which is contrary to his expectations of himself — expectations which originally were those of his parents but which have now become part of his own inner demands. The specific details of development will vary enormously from one family, sub-culture, ethnic group or religion to the next. I am describing the principles which determine development and behaviour. Conscience, ideals, self-regard, guilt, shame, expectations of himself are all constantly in the forefront of the adolescent's life and affect a great deal of his behaviour, but the manner in which he experiences each of these is linked closely to his experiences of childhood. Freud described adolescence partly as a repetition of childhood, but now experienced in a different way from childhood because of the fact that the person has reached physical sexual maturity.

When we try to judge whether a child's development is progressing well or whether there are signs of psychological stress, the areas of his life which we examine are very different from those which would be examined in assessing the development of the adolescent. For the child, our concern would be with such things as bladder and bowel control, food intake and habits, school performance, relationships with friends, the use the child makes of belongings, sleep habits, whether he plays with boys or girls, whether his friends are of his own age or younger or older, whether he can compete with friends while at the same time admire their achievements.

The psychological and social interferences which take place during childhood can severely handicap the child's present and future life. Many children can be very troubled or disturbed but their compliance with outside expectations and standards enables them to get by even though the stress is obvious if one only looks. We are familiar with the 'good' child who is no trouble to anybody, or the quiet child who does as he is told and never complains. But often the child may be failing at school, or he has no friends, or he cries secretly or, worse still, he may be unable to show his distress. When the child reaches adolescence, he may suddenly be confronted with the fact that his earlier ways of dealing with stress are now greater handicaps than ever. The quiet, rather withdrawn or 'good' child, who may have been thought of by his parents as being just the kind of child they wanted, is suddenly faced in adolescence with the fact that the behaviour which brought approval in childhood is no longer of much use to him now. Instead of the approval which he got in childhood, he may now feel isolated, he may begin to realize that others do not want to have much to do with him, and he may have to recognize the distressing fact that some of his thoughts and feelings may be a handicap. The adolescent may find that the excuses of childhood prove to be insufficient because the consequences are much more drastic now — isolation, sadness, feeling that something is wrong with him, feeling that he is a failure socially, or perhaps feeling that his thoughts are abnormal and are frightening to him.

These are some of the reasons why psychological disturbance or breakdown in adolescence sometimes seems to come 'out of the blue'. There is the adolescent who seems to change without apparent reason; or who suddenly commits suicide; or who must be admitted to hospital urgently; or the brilliant child who suddenly fails at school when he reaches adolescence. What we see is a collapse of the earlier ways of meeting various situations of stress. The adolescent is instead faced with the fact that he *is* failing, or that he *is* alone, or that he may be developing abnormally either socially or sexually. The additional disappointment for him is that his parents' approval or reassurance is no longer as effective as it was when he was a child. Now he seeks approval and recognition from his contemporaries, but in order to get this he has to respond or behave in a way which is acceptable to them. Their standards may be different from those of his parents, but

primarily, the approval or disapproval, the feelings of
self-hatred or self-love, come from his own conscience. It is
this which makes the adolescent feel a success or a failure,
'good' or 'no good', worthless or even empty.

Although the foundations for future psychological life are
laid early, it is usually only during the time we call 'latency',
that is, from the age of six or seven to eleven or twelve, that
we can make more sense of danger signs; we may see that the
person's adolescence (and therefore adulthood) will be a time
of more or less straightforward development or a time of
serious trouble.

The withdrawn, shy and perhaps frightened child will
inevitably have trouble in adolescence. The reasons for this
withdrawal or shyness will, of course, also determine the way
it interferes with the person's life at this time. Fred is aged
sixteen — a very unhappy and, potentially, a seriously
disturbed person. His present life is a very lonely and anxious
one, even though he is doing extremely well at school and is
loved very much by his parents who are very concerned about
him. He spends a great deal of time playing chess by himself or
busying himself with various complicated chemical
experiments. During his latency, he was almost invariably 'ill'
on sports day, with near-legitimate excuses such as
stomach-ache, headache, sudden vomiting attacks, or outbursts
of uncontrolled crying. He is still very shy about his own
body, but during his latency it was impossible for him to show
any part of his body. He could not allow himself to be seen
without a shirt and vest. To be seen in the nude was totally
impossible. Fred is having very serious trouble now and will go
on having trouble unless something is done to help him. He
views his body as a source of danger and discomfort, a burden
rather than something with which to be comfortable. It is
difficult to know whether he will become suicidal, but some of
the adolescents who kill themselves or attempt to do so have
histories of feeling their bodies to be something to be ashamed
of and something to fight against, as if they are perpetual
victims of the feelings coming from their bodies. In Fred's case
we can assume that his adolescence will continue to be a time
of great unhappiness. His future life will very likely be one of

isolation, extreme shyness, inability to have a girlfriend, and most likely an inability to marry and live a normal adult life. He may do quite well at his future work, but the other areas of his life will be very difficult.

We often see such signals in childhood which in adolescence become areas of great trouble. I have in mind signals such as truancy, school refusal, compulsive stealing, compulsive lying, as well as the less obvious and quieter forms of trouble such as extreme withdrawal, friendlessness, inability to learn and extreme sadness. These signals are not too difficult to spot, but there are others which are less straightforward, such as the child's choice of friends, the child's overconcern about his school performance, the child's demanding need always to help the teacher and to be loved all the time, or the child's need to be chosen to participate in far too many school activities.

The other forms of behaviour which should be viewed with some concern are the sudden outburst or the sudden breakthrough of a kind of behaviour which is totally out of character with the child's previous way of behaving. Such behaviour may, in reality, turn out to be of no concern — the child may not be feeling well, the parents may have had an argument, the father may have lost his job, or the child's sister may have obtained better school results. More often it may be a sign of potential disturbance, and from the point of view of prevention of future disturbance such behaviour should be investigated and not be dismissed lightly. These are often our first clues to the presence of extreme stress.

In addition to the behaviour discussed earlier which may be viewed as signs of stress in childhood, we would also want to know about actual deprivation in childhood, about physical or mental illness of the parents when the adolescent was a child, about the sudden loss in childhood of somebody or something loved by the child. This information helps us to know more about the extent to which the child may have grown up feeling that he did not have an adult to himself who loved him, as is the case with some children who grow up in institutions; or the extent to which a child's judgement and values are distorted by the fact that he grew up in the presence of a mentally disturbed or ill parent; or the extent to which a child's life was affected by a sudden loss which may have left the child with a feeling that the person or the pet 'didn't love me and went away because I was bad'.

Our understanding of an adolescent's past life enables us to get a clearer picture of the extent of interference in development and functioning which may have existed before he reached physical sexual maturity. It also helps us to know the extent to which it may have been possible to predict that the changes which take place during adolescence would produce additional stress (p. 15 and pp. 24–31).

CHAPTER 3
DANGER SIGNS IN ADOLESCENCE

The variations of normality discussed in Chapter 2 imply a wide range of behaviour or development which can be considered normal, but at the same time, it implies the possibility of abnormal behaviour or development which may also vary in degree and severity.

We know that some adolescents show signs of abnormal stress. Some find ways of dealing with this stress, even though the solutions may interfere seriously with their lives. The adolescent may deny any feelings from his body, and may then get support for this from the group or sect which he has joined and which shares his views. He may find that his athletic ability helps him feel that his body is strong but that he cannot miss one day's training; or he may feel that he cannot risk not studying for one day for fear that he will fail. There are others who, either temporarily or permanently, cannot function in the community, and may have to be admitted to hospital. Some may find the internal stress so unbearable that they are at risk, as can be observed in those who become dependent on drugs or who attempt suicide. There are also those whose link with the outside world is tenuous at best, and who may find it difficult or impossible to differentiate between the 'creations of their own minds' and the outside world; these adolescents show signs of serious mental illness. There are others for whom the term 'breakdown' may be more appropriate: although they are aware of what is going on within themselves and in the outside world, their ability to cope or to function has either stopped or diminished severely, and they cannot manage without care or treatment.

What, then, is mental disturbance or illness in adolescence? What does it mean when we refer to an adolescent as having had a breakdown? How does one know when to begin to be concerned and what to look for?

There are still many conflicting ideas and opinions about mental disturbance and illness, especially in relation to adolescence. Some say that mental illness is an illusion, others that it is really a label which reflects illness in the family members rather than in the adolescent himself. Some people believe that to talk of mental illness in adolescence is unnecessary and unwarranted — that it is simply a euphemism for laziness, work-shyness, antisocial behaviour, or sponging — and that those who view the behaviour of the adolescent as something to be taken seriously may be pampering him and encouraging him to get away with too much. Such a view ignores the fact that there are adolescents who genuinely cannot cope, who are showing signs of serious mental disturbance or illness, and who are in immediate need of help and sometimes of care. It also ignores or rejects the great strides which have taken place in our knowledge about the functioning of the mind and, indirectly, about the prevention and treatment of mental disturbance or illness.

A good deal of argument still goes on amongst those people who work with adolescents about what constitutes a sign of mental disturbance or illness. Some of this argument reflects a genuine difference of view about the meaning of certain forms of behaviour or signs of stress; but it also sometimes contains the idea that there is either no such thing as mental illness in adolescence or that it is potentially harmful to the adolescent to 'label' him as being disturbed or ill. I do not think that labelling, in itself, is the problem; one does not create a problem by recognizing its presence. It is more likely that the opposite is the case; that is, that not to acknowledge the presence of mental disturbance or illness during adolescence can be harmful to the adolescent and can create a great deal of unnecessary additional stress and suffering for him, as well as a great deal of distress for his family. I have seen such an outcome repeatedly.

When I refer to mental disturbance or illness in adolescence I am not referring to the enormous range of behaviour which can be observed in every normal adolescent — the mood swings, the 'crushes', the temporary feelings of hopelessness, the disillusionments, the wild plans, the experimentation with drugs, the fights with teachers, or the disagreements with parents. Every adolescent is temporarily worried whether he or she is good enough, tall enough, pretty enough, intelligent enough, strong enough, feminine enough — and the list can be extended. Most adolescents get through this turmoil and will reach adulthood able to experience pleasure from 'their personal lives. When referring to mental disturbance, illness or breakdown, I have in mind the adolescent who does not get through this turmoil, and who pays a heavy price in emotional terms for the solutions he or she has found or has tried to find as a way of adapting to internal stress.

The fact that many adolescents share similar anxieties and often show similar kinds of behaviour makes it difficult to distinguish between normal, transitory stress and disturbance or illness. For this reason the adolescent's behaviour may not be able to tell us very much on its own. It is the underlying meaning to the adolescent of similar behaviour patterns or reactions which, in one case, may mean that there is nothing to be concerned about and, in another case, may mean that psychological treatment is urgently required.

The problem of assessment is complicated further by the fact that certain behaviour, relationships, emotional reactions or uncharacteristic responses may be appropriate for the young adolescent but not for the older. For example, mutual masturbation early in adolescence need not be a sign of existing or impending disturbance. The same can be true for homosexual relationships during this early period of adolescence; it may be, for the very young adolescent, a means of experimenting with his physically mature body and with the new sexual feelings coming from his own body. But sexual intercourse early in adolescence, either for the boy or the girl, would have to be viewed differently, both in terms of the impact of such an experience on normal development, and of assessment. Sexual intercourse early in adolescence should be viewed with caution; we should not assume that it represents the adolescent's ability to accept his physically mature body. More often, it is either a repudiation of his physically mature body or a sign of severe unhappiness which causes him to give up the privacy of his body. It may also hide a fear that something is wrong with himself, either mentally or physically; the behaviour is then an effort to establish (unsuccessfully) in his mind the belief that he is normal.

Such behaviour will have different meaning for the older adolescent who is nearer to emotional maturity. For the older adolescent, a homosexual relationship is, I think, always a sign of the presence of disturbance. He should by this time have accepted his physically mature body and be able to have heterosexual relationships. During this period the male begins to judge himself as a successful or failed 'man', and the female judges herself as a successful or failed 'woman'. Relationships with one's contemporaries take on a different meaning now; the adolescent is much more prepared psychologically to integrate the experience of sexual intercourse as part of his total personality.

Jane came to see me when she was fourteen because she was unable to concentrate at school. Her parents noticed that she did not get on with her school work and that she seemed to spend a good deal of time on her own. She had a number of friends of her own age, went out with them, and usually reported to her parents that she had a wonderful time wherever she went. They had been somewhat worried about her in the past, but they were unable to specify the cause of their worry. They became very worried, however, when she told them of a friend of hers who had thought of death and who had tried to kill herself. The parents could not imagine which friend she was talking about, and they wondered about the truth of this story, but they, correctly, did not question their daughter. A short time later they suggested to her that she might come to see me. The story itself was a complete fabrication, but it was her way of making her parents anxious about her present state of mind. Her worry about herself became intense when she heard of a girl at school who was lesbian; she then immediately thought that she herself was in danger of being lesbian (something which worries and frightens many girls of this age). She had felt that she must have a boyfriend, and that one of the boys who lived nearby was just right for her. (She herself did not consciously make the link between her fears of being abnormal and her intense wish for a boyfriend.) Jane first had intercourse after she had heard that a friend of hers had done so. To her surprise and disappointment, the experience did not eliminate her feelings of sadness and of being different from other girls, and she became sadder and more anxious. She thought of death as a way out, and she said that this would solve so many problems

at the same time — her extreme shame and guilt, her feeling that her parents would love her more if she were dead, and the feeling that if she were dead she would not have to continue to be preoccupied with her worry that she was developing abnormally. She told me that she often cried secretly and felt that she was 'just nothing', that her friends might think of her as dirty, and that there was nothing to look forward to.

In psychological terms, Jane's fear of being abnormal had made her choose to have intercourse before she was mentally ready. This was her way of reassuring herself that she was normal. In addition, her early sexual experience had taken away from her the experience of being alone. It was as if the process of coming to terms with her physically mature body had been speeded up. It also made her feel that her body perpetually made her do things for which she then hated herself, with the accompanying feeling that her body was her enemy. Early sexual intercourse was certainly not a sign of her normality, but of the presence of extreme anxiety with which she coped temporarily by behaving in a way which could be harmful to her future development.

John, aged eighteen, came to see me because he said he had been feeling depressed. He was a big person physically, and rather handsome. When he began to describe why he had come, he interrupted his story and interjected that perhaps there was no purpose in having come at all because he got depressed very seldom and, in any case, he had been told by a friend that he could go to his doctor who could help him with antidepressant pills. When I asked him about his sadness, he said he felt this way mainly at weekends. He then stopped talking of his depression, and began to talk of a friend who had been admitted to hospital because he had attempted to kill himself. He felt shocked when he heard the news, and said he felt very guilty for not having taken his friend seriously in the past. He was then able to tell me of his own thoughts of wanting to die, of often feeling that there was not much to life. He described his very depressed household — his father had died of cancer when John was aged ten, and now he lived alone with his mother who had a part-time job in a shop near their home. I could have dismissed John's depression as a reaction to this situation, but this would have been a mistake.

Although his thoughts of death concerned me very much, I became more concerned about his mental state when he mentioned that he had recently been spending a great deal of time alone in his room looking in the mirror to see if his face was changing, and that he had to go on doing this to assure himself that this was not happening. His story contained many details of his lack of friends, his tendency to give up and find excuses for not leaving the house, reading for hours at a time, and finding a variety of excuses for not going to the parties to which he had been invited by schoolfriends. He told me that he worried that there might be something seriously wrong with him because he masturbated every day. This had been worrying him for some years, but he never felt able to ask anybody whether there really was anything to worry about. In a subsequent interview, he could tell me that it was not only the masturbation which had been worrying him, but also the fact that during masturbation he often thought of touching other boys. He felt convinced that there was something seriously wrong, but was too ashamed to seek help. He was frightened that if he sought help he might be told he was mad.

Many adolescents are concerned about their bodies, about the normality or abnormality of masturbation, and that if people knew their thoughts they might be considered abnormal. Even though frequent masturbation is not in itself a sign of disturbance, it is quite common for adolescents to worry that it is a sign of existing or impending abnormality; but John was describing something else. He was saying, in terms of psychological development, that he had begun to withdraw from his friends, and that he had become preoccupied with his body and its changes to the point that he could not really think of anything else. His fear of being homosexual had gone beyond the normal fear that many adolescents share; for him it had got to the point that he had begun to stay away from people. His depression was now no longer an example of normal adolescent depression. Instead it was a reflection of a hatred of his own body and a feeling that he was abnormal. Had this been prevalent when he was aged thirteen or fourteen, that is, had he been concerned about his body and how it was developing, or that he masturbated more than he wanted to, I might have been less concerned even though there may have been some cause for worry. Now, at the age of eighteen, these concerns had become overconcerns, and had resulted in John's isolation and in his acceptance of the fact that there was something wrong and perhaps irreversible. Developmentally, he had not progressed towards adulthood, or more specifically, there had been little or no change since he was aged fourteen. In fact, the lack of any move forward in his psychological development for the past four years could be considered a sign of potential danger. His physically mature body felt foreign to him, his friends were seen primarily as constant reminders that there was something wrong with him, and the view he had of himself was that he was not only a failed man but an abnormal one.

Danger signs in development

The most important single factor which can be of help to us in deciding on the seriousness of stress which may be present in the adolescent's life is how the adolescent deals with the stress. One way of deciding this is to look at the functioning of the whole personality, that is, at the manner in which the adolescent deals with stress in various situations. Such an overall view of the adolescent's life makes it possible to see in which areas of functioning any interferences may lie, as well as to what extent these interferences have hindered or halted his move towards normal adulthood.

When trying to decide whether behaviour falls within the wide range of variations of normality, or whether it should be viewed as a sign of the presence of mental disturbance or illness, the criteria which follow can be considered as guides. The nine criteria enable us to view the adolescent in different situations and, considered together, they give us a more comprehensive picture of the functioning of the personality.

Is the pull back to forms of behaviour common in childhood so strong that there is the danger of giving up the effort or the wish to adopt more adult behaviour?
This childish behaviour is often described, more technically, as 'regression' and 'satisfactions obtained from regressive

behaviour'. We know that every adolescent will get some
satisfaction from this kind of behaviour and that everyone, to
some extent, hesitates to give up this earlier behaviour. It is,
therefore, helpful to know whether he can give up most of
these kinds of behaviour for the more appropriate activities of
adolescence. Sometimes he holds on to these earlier forms of
behaviour because they continue to offer him satisfaction; or
it may be that he is frightened of more adult behaviour. For
example, he may want to be cared for, looked after and loved
by his mother as if he were still a little child, rather than give
this up for more adult ways of gaining love and respect. Or, he
may become ill, stay in bed, and indirectly demand that he
continue to be cared for as if he were still a child.

**Is the adolescent's behaviour so rigid that it does not, or
cannot, allow for temporary relaxation of his demands for his
own self-control?**
In contrast to the previous criterion, there are some
adolescents who are unable, even temporarily, to give up the
more 'grown-up' forms of behaviour. Such adolescents are
unable to risk any changes whatsoever either in their own or
others' behaviour usually with the result that they become
deadened to thoughts or feelings. They feel endangered by any
feeling of which they are not in total control. They see their
bodies, therefore, as a constant source of danger to them. An
example is of the male adolescent who cannot masturbate; or
who cannot allow himself to like another adolescent, because
this might make him 'behave badly'; or who constantly
criticizes other young people for their behaviour, but who
insists on isolating himself and being only interested in his
studies or his hobby.

**Do social relationships help to perpetuate childhood
relationships, or do they assist the adolescent in attaining
adulthood?**
Even though many adolescents appear to choose their friends
in a haphazard way, they actually select them very carefully.
There is the adolescent who can be friends only with people
who admire him, or who bully him, or humiliate him; he will
tend to stay away from those with whom he has to compete or
those whom he feels to be better than he is. Another will have

a large number of friends; for him the choice is based on the common wish to grow up and support one another in times of stress. The group will use one another as confidantes, and they may often discuss private worries, with the knowledge that they will be taken seriously and will be helped. Some, however, are unable to risk this kind of 'equal intimacy'; instead they choose much younger people, or someone who needs caring for; or they may be unable to risk having any friends at all. An adolescent boy whom I knew always chose the smaller boys who admired and loved him. He imagined being their hero, and he felt temporarily that he was in charge. At the same time, he was unable to go out with girls, he secretly hated the other boys at school for being much more competent, and when alone he felt distressed and worthless. For a while he could pretend that he was as good as the rest of them, but as he grew older this pretence proved useless and he became isolated and severely depressed.

Do friends and contemporaries assume greater importance in the life of the adolescent than the parents do?

As the adolescent gets older he should be able to feel that his thoughts, feelings and decisions are becoming independent of those of the parents. This is not to say that he should be expected or encouraged to be antagonistic towards his family, or that he should not have feelings for them. It is more a change of attitude to the family, rather than an aggressive declaration of not caring. He should begin to be more concerned about the opinions, attitudes and feelings of his friends. The boy or girl who, at the age of eighteen or nineteen, is crippled by the inability to hurt his or her parents' feelings when it may be temporarily appropriate to disregard them is, in fact, completely dependent upon them. There is the adolescent, for example, who can choose as friends only those who are approved of by his parents; or whose choice of work cannot be different from what his parents expect; or who cannot have attitudes which are different from those of his parents. Dependence on or independence from the parents refers to the adolescent's emotional relationship with them, and to the inner freedom or lack of freedom in relation to them.

Does the adolescent have the ability to express or experience appropriate feelings, or is there a marked discrepancy between an event and the way in which he reacts to it?
Some adolescents are unable to express certain kinds of feelings; it is as if they are never angry, sad or happy. There are others who seem to have one or two predictable reactions to various situations; it is as if they are frightened of feeling or showing any emotion other than these one or two.

Certain kinds of important situations or events — a disappointment, a temporary failure, an illness or death of somebody important — normally bring about specific reactions in the adolescent. Inappropriate feelings or those which are out of context should be taken as a sign of danger. An example is the adolescent who is describing a problem which is of concern to him and who casually mentions that his father died two weeks ago. He refers to this as if it were incidental to his life. Normally we would expect to observe some signs of sadness and mourning for the lost parent; if he is unable to experience such feelings he will not be able, over a period of time, to adjust emotionally to the fact that his father has died.

The inappropriate reaction or feeling can be observed in a variety of situations — the boy who fails an important examination and who cannot show disappointment; the boy or girl whose parent is very ill but who 'forgets' to go home from school until very late; or the girl whose boyfriend has given her up and who, because of her inability to experience feelings of sadness or rejection, will immediately try to find another boyfriend.

Is there any interference in the adolescent's ability to judge and distinguish other people's reactions from the creations of his own mind?
This is an important criterion in assessing the presence of severe mental disturbance. All of us have tendencies or characteristics which affect the manner in which we view the outside world; we may be somewhat suspicious or shy, or we may generally feel anxious about things when there is no real reason to feel this way. But this is different from the person

who feels convinced that people are plotting against him, or who feels shy to the point of never leaving home, or who is convinced that people 'can read his mind'.

An adolescent girl, for example, came to see me, and when I asked her what was worrying her replied that there was no need to go into detail because I not only knew what might be worrying her, but she was convinced that I could read her mind simply by looking at her. She said she was convinced that everybody could read her thoughts, and she knew that people were plotting against her. Clearly, she was showing signs of severe mental disturbance because she could not now differentiate between what was coming from outside herself and what was a fabrication of her own mind.

As discussed previously, every adolescent is normally concerned about his or her changing body, how it looks, and how he or she feels about it. This preoccupation is quite normal, even if it tends to disturb the parents who may feel that too much of their son's or daughter's time is being taken up with 'trying to look nice'. But when the adolescent begins to feel convinced that something drastic is happening or may happen to his body, or that there are some ominous changes taking place in it, then this should be viewed as a sign of psychological disturbance. An example is the adolescent who is preoccupied with spots on his face. One person will normally be embarrassed about this, but will continue to function — he will attend school, go out with friends and so on, even though he may feel awkward; another may isolate himself completely, refuse to go to school or work, and may believe that everybody is laughing at him. It is when the adolescent reacts in a way which shows that he has lost, or is losing, the ability to make the division between what is actually going on and what he imagines and believes is going on, that we should view his behaviour or reactions as a sign of the presence of serious disturbance. The most extreme interferences in functioning can be seen in schizophrenia, where the person is no longer able to know that the distortions come completely from his own mind. Here we see what is commonly referred to as a break with reality.

What is the adolescent's attitude to the future? Does he see it
as something to look forward to or as something dreadful or
frightening?

His attitude to the future reflects the extent to which he is
able to picture himself as an adult, and whether he is able to
begin to take into account his abilities as well as his
limitations. Adolescence is, normally, a time which should
carry with it some excitement as well as some apprehension
about the future, but there are some adolescents who either

do not care, or who see the future as something awful. This should be viewed as a sign of underlying depression or as a reflection of the adolescent's fear that he will fail, both socially and sexually, as an adult. In addition, as the adolescent gets older, he should begin to be able to assess more realistically his personal strengths and limitations. An extreme example of an adolescent's inability to make such an assessment is the following:

Tom was aged nineteen when he came to see me. He had recently given up his job, and insisted that he must study medicine. He did not have any O- or A-levels and was now working as a clerk, but he thought that he might be accepted at a medical school if he applied. He spent all of his free time reading medical textbooks, and did not have any friends; he felt he could not spare the time because he had to acquire all the necessary knowledge. When he did enquire at a medical school about studying medicine and was told that he could not be considered, he gave up his job and stayed at home because he felt there was no longer any purpose in trying to do anything at all.

There are some adolescents who temporarily share a common attitude of the future. This is sometimes seen among adolescents living together in a large group or in a commune. While in this milieu, they seem to function well, and their loneliness or feeling of worthlessness is temporarily removed; adolescents who may be experiencing extreme stress feel that, while they are among others who share the same views and the same attitudes about the future, they are getting on well and they 'never felt better'. They may have been very depressed and isolated in the past, but they may now feel that everything is working out well and that the future does not matter. They are for the time being a great help to one another, but they do not remove the causes of the depression or of the vulnerability to future mental disturbance.

Are there certain kinds of thoughts which seriously impair the adolescent's ability to function, or is he able to cope with various frightening thoughts without giving up the wish to become an adult?

Adolescence is normally characterized by weird, frightening and disturbing thoughts about aspects of his life which are now of great concern: the body, intercourse, masturbation, or relationships in general with the opposite sex. Adolescents vary considerably in their reactions to these thoughts. Some have frightening and disturbing thoughts without feeling that these are signs of madness or abnormality. Others do not allow themselves to have any such thoughts because they regard them as bad, dangerous or even dirty; if for any reason they do, they feel ashamed and guilty and feel that they deserve to be punished or rejected.

In masturbation, for example, it is normal to have thoughts which may seem childish and which may make the adolescent feel guilty or ashamed. Some can deal with these feelings without worrying that they are going mad, but others feel so frightened and threatened that they are unable to allow any thought into their minds which is not under complete control. They may go so far as to renounce any feelings which come from their bodies, and may try to behave as if they do not have any feelings at all. Such people cannot succeed in integrating their physically mature bodies with the view they have of themselves; their sexual identity must therefore be distorted.

Is the adolescent able to feel that his actions are determined by himself rather than by somebody or something outside himself?
One important change which accompanies the move into adolescence is the increased use of actions. Actions can be a way of dealing with inner tension; they can be a way of expressing feelings; they can act as a substitute for thinking; they can be a sign of the person's effort to gain control over a part of himself of which he is frightened. Some feel able consciously to control their actions; others feel compelled to use actions. They may consciously feel that they have to do certain things, that is, that actions 'occur' rather than that they are the initiators of these actions. Others again may feel responsible for their actions but, at the same time, feel that they cannot control them or have regard for the consequences.

We can see the use of actions, on the one hand, in sports, dancing, the acquisition of skills, and on the other hand, in delinquent behaviour, fighting, some illegitimate pregnancies and so on. For example, the adolescent girl who has grown up with the belief that she is illegitimate may have to become pregnant; through her actions she tries to deal with this fact or fantasy by having to repeat what she felt happened to her. There are some who are not able to use actions for various forms of expression or thought, but who may suddenly do something which expresses everything they feel about themselves. For example, there is the boy who is very polite, good at his studies, slightly withdrawn, never any real trouble to anybody, who suddenly leaves university to get a job as a labourer 'because that's all I'm good for'.

These criteria, in addition to creating a picture which reflects the adolescent's overall functioning, have a preventive value because they make it possible to spot danger signs which otherwise might be allowed to pass unnoticed.

To some extent, one of the problems for assessment is that the adolescent's life is divided into a variety of roles — the student, the apprentice, the club member, the child in the family and so on. The concern of any one person for the adolescent may then revolve primarily around the responsibility each one may have — as a parent, a teacher, a doctor, a youth leader, or a personnel officer. Although such a division may be inevitable, the danger is that, unless we have a broader view of what adolescence is about, we could easily make the mistake of thinking that all is well at a time when the adolescent may be in present or potential danger as regards his social and psychological health.

Gary, aged eighteen, came to see me because he had recently made a suicide attempt by taking an overdose of sleeping pills. He had been admitted to hospital after the attempt and was discharged within two days. His doctor then prescribed more anti-depressant pills and told Gary to get in touch with him if he felt depressed again. Luckily, Gary's father did not accept the doctor's or the hospital's way of dealing with the crisis. When Gary came to see me he told me that he had felt depressed and isolated for some time. He had recently won a scholarship to a university, and for a short time believed that this new life would make all the difference. In fact, soon after he got to university he felt more isolated than ever before. His outstanding academic achievements made his tutor, as had happened previously with his teacher, feel that he was getting on very well and his suicide attempt was a shock to everybody, but even then some people clearly tried to deny that there was anything wrong. When I talked with his parents, they described their own reactions to his development as follows: 'He never had many friends. Sometimes he might come home with another boy, but usually a friend would last for a week or so. Most of the time he was on his own. We ourselves never knew much about mental trouble so we didn't think there was too much wrong if our boy stayed at home. Mind you, he didn't do much besides studying all the time, but we didn't want to interfere too much, because everybody said he was an outstanding boy and they all had high hopes for him.' Gary's disturbance had been allowed to pass for a long time because he had been doing well and he was no trouble to anybody. His suffering was 'quiet'.

The presence of one or more danger signs can tell us that interference in development exists or may exist in the future, but this does not answer totally the question of how severe the mental disturbance or illness may be. Such an assessment, however, is critical from a preventive point of view, as it should influence the decision about the nature and extent of help which the adolescent needs. The next chapter concentrates on describing mental disturbance, illness and breakdown in adolescence.

CHAPTER 4
MENTAL DISTURBANCE, ILLNESS AND BREAKDOWN IN ADOLESCENCE

Most adolescents manage to cope with what is commonly referred to as 'adolescent upheaval'. For those that do not, however 'sudden' some disturbance or illness or breakdown seems to be, it always has a history and is not sudden at all. This has been described in the previous chapter.

We are now much less ready to describe the adolescent as lazy or delinquent, nor do we any longer disregard the fact that an adolescent has no friends, or must always be first in the class in every subject, or is so good that he or she is no trouble to anybody. We look much more cautiously and carefully for early signs of mental disturbance or breakdown. Although statistics are still inexact about the incidence of mental illness, it is acknowledged that at least one in eight adults will spend some time in a psychiatric hospital during their lives. This means that in a school of 500, about sixty to seventy will, in their adult lives, spend a period in hospital because of mental disturbance or illness. But all that such a statistic says simply is that one in eight adults shows behaviour which is **acknowledged** as requiring admission to hospital. This figure is not necessarily an accurate reflection of the extent of the mental disturbance or illness in the community, because there are those who can cope, who somehow get by, but who are within themselves desperately unhappy and possibly seriously disturbed people.

If we are concerned about an adolescent, we can ask ourselves a simple question: 'What kind of person will he or she be in ten years time?' This question contains a number of assumptions about mental development. An important one is that we can often see early signs of stress or serious mental disturbance already present in adolescence, and this same stress will, in adulthood, produce a much more defined and established picture. We know from the study and treatment of seriously disturbed adults that such an outcome always means their preceding development must have been seriously interfered with and they must have shown signs of existing or pending trouble.

In adolescence, however, such signs do not themselves enable us to know how severe the interference is. We know that some react to stress by temporarily behaving in ways which make us think that actual disturbance or illness is present, even though this need not be so. Some do feel temporarily overwhelmed by stress and they react in ways which show that they are not able to cope. Others behave as if they are not responding at all to the stress.

For assessment, therefore, there are four categories which imply different degrees and quality of interference or damage to mental functioning. They can be defined as follows:

Normal, temporary stress is the result of the new demands being made on the adolescent — demands which come both from within himself and from his friends and contemporaries. Such stress may interfere temporarily in his day-to-day life, but he is still able to function well.

Mental disturbance (neurotic disturbance) refers to established interference in a person's development, which still leaves intact the ability to cope with all or some of the demands coming from within himself and from the outside world; the adolescent is still able to manage at school or work, but at a reduced level. He can differentiate between what is going on outside himself and the 'creations of his mind'. For example, he may feel that people are looking at him, but he knows that this is not really happening; he can acknowledge that he feels shy and perhaps suspicious, and that it is this which makes him feel people are looking at him.

Mental illness (psychosis) means that the adolescent has lost contact with outside reality; he is not able to differentiate between what is going on outside himself and the 'creations of his mind'. The different forms of schizophrenia and depressive psychosis fit into this category of illness.

Adolescent breakdown is, I believe, a sub-category of mental illness which, although it may contain many unknowns, distinguishes established mental illness and illness which may be a sign of the temporary overwhelming of the personality.

Each of these four categories will now be described in greater detail.

Normal, temporary stress

The adolescent is able to function well, even though there may be signs of stress. Any interference in functioning is of a temporary nature which is due to developmental stress and will diminish and disappear as the adolescent gets older. The adolescent may feel depressed, angry, or anxious that he is not doing well enough. He may one day have definite plans for his future, which are then completely discarded. He may doubt his ability and feel that his parents expect too much of him; he may temporarily not want to see his friends; he may worry that girls do not care much for him; he may even sometimes behave as a child. But while these doubts and anxieties exist, he is still able to function well at school or work, with friends, and with his family. The experiences in which he involves himself help him to progress in his development.

The nine criteria which are discussed in Chapter 3 can be helpful in deciding the extent of interference, whether it seems to be of a temporary nature, or whether it is more permanent and fixed.

Mental disturbance in adolescence (neurotic disturbance)

The adolescent is able to function, even though the solutions which he finds to the developmental problems of adolescence result in a degree of maladaptation which may endanger his future ability to get satisfaction from his work and personal life. I have in mind the adolescent, for example, who may have difficulty, or find it impossible, to change the relationship with his parents, and reaches adulthood unable to make other close relationships; or he may find unsatisfactory ways of dealing with his physically mature body, and feel and behave as if his body is still the property of his mother.

The interference in development can be observed in a variety of ways; here again the danger signs which are elaborated in Chapter 3 can be of use. There is the adolescent who is unable to criticize his parents for fear that he may hurt them; who is friendless; who is obsessed by his body and its functioning, but who is nevertheless unable to masturbate; the girl who cannot allow herself to be touched sexually by her boyfriend because she is frightened that this will harm her in some way; the boy who cannot allow himself to have any feelings whatsoever, because to do so would mean risking loss of self-control; the girl who feels constantly depressed, even though she feels that everything is going well in her life; the boy who feels that he may develop abnormally even though he is aware that there is no cause to be concerned; the boy who suddenly drops out of university; the girl who is unable to keep a job. This interference may be described as neurotic; that is, it is due to inner conflict which results in a degree of deadlock in development.

The extent of mental disturbance in adolescence may vary considerably. In some instances, the degree of interference is very limited and can be described as 'simple neurotic' disturbance; the inner conflict does not interfere seriously in the adolescent's life, but his functioning is at a reduced level. In 'serious neurotic' disturbance there is extreme interference in development or there is long-standing and more permanent deadlock and interruption in functioning. In both cases, however, these adolescents do not lose touch with the external world; they continue to be able to differentiate between the reactions of the outside world and the creations of their own minds.

When assessing the extent of disturbance it is important to keep in mind the person's age and the appropriateness of the behaviour to that age. The boy of thirteen who cannot allow himself to masturbate may, for example, be showing a sign of temporary (transitory) stress without its necessarily being a sign of established disturbance; however, if this boy is still unable to masturbate at eighteen or nineteen it should be viewed as a sign of established disturbance because this conveys the adolescent's fear of his own sexual feelings or of his thoughts. It may also be a sign that the adolescent is trying to disown his sexually mature body. The girl of fourteen who finds herself unable to go to a party, who feels shy with boys, and who believes that she is not as pretty as other girls, may be showing signs of temporary stress; however, if this girl is still unable to go to parties or allow herself to go out with boys at eighteen or nineteen, then this should be viewed as a sign of established disturbance because it may mean that she cannot cope with her fears of what can happen to her as a 'woman', or that she may be trying to keep her self-control by remaining a child.

Mental illness (psychosis) and adolescent breakdown

Mental illness and adolescent breakdown can be discussed together because they have some common characteristics. They both must be taken very seriously because they reflect severe damage to mental functioning and because the adolescent is in immediate need of help and sometimes of care as well. In both, the adolescent's sense of reality may be interfered with to such a degree that his life may be in danger.

The differentiation between mental illness and adolescent breakdown is a critical one, because the kind of help or care needed may be different for the two categories, and the outcome of treatment as well as the future outlook for the person may not be the same.

Mental illness refers here to a state where the adolescent has lost touch with reality, where the creations of his own mind are felt to be determined by, or operating in, the outside world. This kind of reaction is sometimes also observed in breakdown, but the difference is, I think, that in mental illness the disorder is much more established and fixed and there are few, if any, areas of functioning which are not in some way affected by the illness. There may also be signs of thought and speech disorder, disorders of memory, and disturbance of movement: the person may lose the link between words and their meaning; he may remember things which may not have actually taken place; or he may not be able to remember what has just occurred. It often seems impossible to raise any doubt in the adolescent suffering from mental illness about the creations of his own mind. He is convinced that what his mind is creating is true. This can be observed in such mental illnesses as schizophrenia and depressive psychosis.

The development of mental illness is something about

which we know little. Parents have often asked me, 'Why has my son developed this way?' This question often also contains the parents' self-accusation and belief that they went wrong somewhere and that they might have been able to have prevented such an outcome. The answer at this stage in our understanding of mental illness must be 'We do not know.' Of course, the parents' own personalities do participate actively in a child's future development, but this does not mean that a parent has done something 'wrong' which has produced mental illness in his son or daughter.

Very often, people say that mental illness is inherited or is determined by various aspects of the adolescent's history — for example, there may have been some mental illness in the family; or the adolescent may have had a very difficult upbringing. Nevertheless I do not believe that such descriptions or such 'facts' explain mental illness. It is very important, however, in assessing the extent of disturbance to differentiate between established mental illness in the adolescent (as in schizophrenia or depressive psychosis) and behaviour which the adolescent has unconsciously copied from a mentally disturbed or ill parent. Many adolescents describe behaviour which resembles mental illness, and express their fear that they are ill because their parent(s) has been or is mentally disturbed or ill, but further description of their behaviour, or their functioning in general, confirms that they have identified with a mentally disturbed or ill parent and have adopted reactions which are similar to those of the parent. These adolescents may in fact be disturbed, but they are not mentally ill in the sense described earlier. There is no evidence to show that people 'inherit' a mental illness or are more vulnerable to mental illness because of its presence in another member of the family. A history of mental disturbance or illness in the family often plays on the adolescent's fear that he may be mentally ill or that there is something wrong psychologically, and he may unconsciously show behaviour which is then felt by him to be a confirmation that there is something wrong with him.

Many people still believe that mental illness can be spotted easily, and that the person shows very extreme behaviour and is obviously 'mad'. This is far from what happens. Mental illness in adolescence need not be loud or obvious at all, but can be present in a quiet way. In such a case the adolescent may be completely taken up with his own fantasy world and, for example, may feel that he must do certain things because 'the voice in me says I have to do it'; or he may be convinced that he is Christ and that he must behave accordingly; or that the world's troubles are his fault, and that he deserves to be punished; or that he must not eat food offered him because he will be poisoned by it. He may lock himself in his room because he 'knows' that people are after him and he must protect himself from them. A girl may 'know' that her body is really a male body, and that she must protect herself from everybody because 'they' will say that this is not so. Here the person's mental processes are no longer intact, and the interference or damage to mental functioning has gone far beyond interrupting normal development. In such instances the link with reality has been lost — the creations of his mind are accepted by him as true, and he has no ability at that point to doubt these 'creations'.

Uncharacteristic reactions or odd behaviour may have to be taken seriously, but need not be a sign of mental illness. One must be very careful in assessment: it is obviously important to recognize mental illness when it is there, however unobtrusive it may appear to be, but it is also important not to assess on the basis of behaviour alone and to label the adolescent as showing signs of mental illness when this may not be the case at all. Although denial of the presence of illness can be harmful, wrong assessment can be a terrible burden for the adolescent and his family, and it is something which is very difficult for the adolescent to overcome in the future.

Adolescent breakdown, as opposed to established mental illness (psychosis), refers to mental functioning where the reactions are not necessarily the outcome of latent mental illness, even though the ability to function may be as severely disrupted. However, the assessment of adolescent breakdown implies that the disruption may be due to an overwhelming of the personality

The creations of their own minds feel as real for these adolescents as for those suffering from mental illness, but the primary difference is that adolescent breakdown refers to a more sudden and possibly temporary disruption. These people will almost certainly have been vulnerable before adolescence, but certain experiences in adolescence may overwhelm them, resulting in a halt in the ability to function or in a temporary break with reality. These experiences can come from the special inner stresses of adolescence, or from the outside world. Even though these adolescents may seem to have lost the link with reality, they are at least partially aware that the creations of their own minds are not a reflection of what is really going on. They feel overwhelmed by the feelings which they experience, and respond as if they have temporarily lost control of being able to do anything about them. It is as if they feel they have no alternative but to respond in a mad way. They are often very frightened and confused by their responses, but at the same time they feel temporarily unable to respond in any other way.

Many adolescents present such a picture of confusion and disorganization, and might wrongly be described as suffering from mental illness. I have seen adolescents who have been overwhelmed by a bad drug trip, by feelings which they believe to be out of their control, or by external events such as separation, divorce or the death of a parent. They find themselves unable to cope, they may feel they are mad or going mad, or that they will lose control.

Attempted suicide in adolescence is certainly a sign of breakdown, if not of actual mental illness. I think it is a serious error to consider attempted suicide in adolescence as a sign of temporary crisis or as a wish simply to get attention. The adolescent who attempts suicide will often use an event (rejection by a boy- or girlfriend, failure in an examination, a homosexual experience) as a final confirmation of his already existing feeling that he is bad, worthless, abnormal or that his body is the source of all his evil. He may be aware that he thinks these things and he may know that they are not really true, but an event of some kind makes him temporarily believe them and he will be overwhelmed by the feelings about

himself and his body. He responds in a completely unreal way, by attacking his body and endangering his life.

Other signs of established mental disturbance

Although it is important to guard against drawing conclusions about the presence of mental disturbance or of its severity from an adolescent's behaviour, there are certain forms of behaviour which should be viewed as being more than a danger sign. Some behaviour clearly indicates that the stress is not transitory and that, if not treated, the adolescent will almost certainly reach adulthood with signs of mental abnormality.

I refer to such behaviour as transvestitism; homosexuality in older adolescents; compulsive over-eating which results in obesity; anorexia nervosa; addiction to drugs; self-injury;

established symptoms such as bedwetting, stuttering, the
various phobias such as fear of animals, fear of leaving the
house, fear of travelling on trains or in cars; compulsive or
repeated delinquencies, including stealing, 'breaking and
entering'; compulsive gambling; repeated drunkenness;
inability to work. Such behaviour does not convey how severe
the disturbance is, but it can tell us that there are definite
signs of the presence of interference in development. In these
instances the person's adult life cannot be a normal one in the
psychological sense unless he is treated.

CHAPTER 5
HELP FOR MENTALLY DISTURBED AND ILL ADOLESCENTS

Although the mentally ill adolescent requires care and treatment which takes the severity of his illness into account, it is no longer appropriate for us to confine our thinking or efforts to helping only those who are obviously mentally ill or who cannot function any longer. Consequently, the definition of what constitutes help or treatment can be extended to include a variety of forms of intervention.

We should not assume that whatever is done for an adolescent is either treatment or help; there are times when some kinds of help are useless or even harmful. Advice such as 'pull yourself together' or reassurance such as 'you will grow out of it' can be harmful because it may deter him from seeking appropriate help. This can have serious consequences because the adolescent is at a point in his development where he will soon have to make decisions which will affect his whole future life. There is the adolescent, for example, who leaves school suddenly because he feels that he is unable to cope with forthcoming exams. Instead of being helped with this fear of failing, he is allowed to leave and then gets a job which is far below his potential. Another example is the girl who is expelled from school for taking drugs; the fact that she complains of feeling 'dead' and is obviously seriously depressed is completely disregarded. Or there is the girl who becomes pregnant, agrees to a termination but who becomes very depressed, and two months later becomes pregnant again. Instead of her depression and feelings of abnormality being recognized, she is simply considered to be a 'terrible burden'.

Some who are in need of help will, because of their fear of what may be wrong, or because of their feeling of isolation or confusion, look for people to advise or to counsel them, or will go to their doctor for reassurance. Temporarily, such help may act as a relief, but in the long run it strengthens their denial that there is anything wrong, and it may make them feel that nothing can be done or that no one can do anything effectively to help. They go on living with their disturbance, often feeling that people have let them down.

Some people are not necessarily mentally ill or suffering from breakdown, but there is no doubt that they show signs of disturbance and of interference in their development which is serious enough to warrant professional assessment and perhaps help or treatment. Whether they get it depends on a variety of factors, some of which have to do with the adolescent himself and some of which may be quite fortuitous.

What do adolescents want help for?

The ways in which adolescents express or describe their feeling that something may be wrong with them vary a great deal. They can take various forms: worry about feeling depressed, the inability to get on with boys or girls, the inability to keep a job, worry about being abnormal in some way, the fear of madness, over-eating, behaving in an uncontrolled way, a belief that there is something wrong with their bodies, feeling guilty about masturbation and worrying that they have harmed themselves in some way, friendlessness, trouble with parents, drug-taking, an inability to express what is wrong but a feeling that 'things are not going right', feeling that they must be mentally ill because one of their parents behaves oddly, and so on.

Some find it difficult to talk about their problems, or they may not know how best to describe what is worrying them, but if an adolescent says he is worried about himself, he should be listened to carefully and his worries should be taken seriously, no matter how simply or undramatically he talks about them.

Those adolescents who seek help represent only a minority of the young people in the community who are vulnerable. Some may have recognized that something is not right, and they try to do something about it. Some seek help under protest because of the pressure put upon them by a parent, a teacher or doctor. Others, even though they recognize the extent of their need for help, may not want to go to a clinic, their doctor, or a psychiatric out-patient service, because these services are too closely associated with actual mental illness. For them, such a visit represents an acceptance by them that there is something seriously wrong; so they stay away.

There are obviously many reasons why the adolescent wants to avoid or postpone seeking help, but if he does decide to seek help or treatment, he and his parents will need to know how to go about locating the services and what form of help or treatment is likely to be appropriate in his case.

Appropriate help or treatment

Some adolescents are in need of help in understanding certain stresses, even though these stresses do not reflect serious mental disturbance; others need help or treatment to remove the interferences which exist in their present lives and which reflect vulnerability to more serious disturbances later on. Others break down; they are no longer able to cope and are in need of care and treatment; others are mentally ill to the extent that they need care over a period of time. Others are vulnerable largely because of detrimental family or living circumstances; for them, help may have to include help to move to a hostel, a change of job, or a change in their course of study. Others are seriously at risk and, for them, help or treatment must include arrangements whereby they can be protected from their wish to harm or to kill themselves.

The severity of the disturbance should be the primary factor in deciding on the kind of help or treatment which is needed, but the attitude of the adolescent to his disturbance, the attitude of the parents to help or treatment, the environmental circumstances, the various commitments which the person may have at school or work, the urgency of the need for treatment, must all be taken into account.

A guiding principle in helping or treating the adolescent is to try and create some insight and understanding of the meaning of his stress or disturbance, and to enable him to feel that he is no longer the victim of unknown forces which determine the direction of his life. The adolescent who is experiencing trouble feels alone and isolated, and is often frightened by the fact that his life is developing in ways which are contrary to what he wants. Help or treatment which creates insight and understanding also gives the adolescent the feeling that he has an ally in his fight against his problems and this, in turn, creates a feeling of hope that something can be done to help him.

Those forms of help or treatment which do not do this can be frightening, discouraging, or humiliating, and can remove the feeling of any hope of change. They increase the sense of isolation and helplessness. Treatment which depends exclusively on environmental changes or drugs or electric shock is contrary to what is needed by the disturbed or vulnerable or ill adolescent. Drugs can be of assistance in enabling the very disturbed or ill to become more accessible to contact and perhaps to treatment. This is quite different, however, from viewing drugs, hostel or hospital care as 'the treatment'; they are, or may be, part of the ancillary services needed, but these measures themselves do not constitute treatment of mental disturbance, illness or breakdown.

The adolescent who is mentally ill presents very special problems of care and treatment. Psychotic illness in adolescence, that is, when the person's sense of reality has been totally disrupted, is not yet well understood. Some professional people believe that the adolescent who is mentally ill can respond to treatment which produces insight and understanding; there are others who advocate various drugs or electric-shock treatment. The lack of knowledge about mental illness and the effectiveness of treatment should make professional people very careful in promising something which may end in disappointment. Even though the effectiveness of the treatment of the mentally ill adolescent may be uncertain, the need for help and care is urgent. The availability of hospital facilities where the adolescent can live without feeling humiliated or forgotten, and the availability of various community facilities (hostels, special day-care centres, specially chosen schools or places of employment) for those who can manage outside a hospital environment, are of great importance in enabling him to function to some extent. However, caring for or helping him in his day-to-day life is in no way synonymous with removing the causes of the illness.

Parents and the mentally disturbed and ill adolescent

The parents of the mentally disturbed or ill adolescent are also experiencing a crisis in their lives. Their first reaction to the awareness that there may be something wrong with their son or daughter is often to avoid thinking about it, but their ability to acknowledge that something is or may be wrong can be reassuring and helpful to their child.

Some parents who are extremely worried about their son or daughter do not know what to do, what to say, or how to behave. It is as if they do not want to create more worry than already exists. Many feel that their son's or daughter's problems are their fault — they feel that they may not have brought them up correctly, that they have failed in some way as parents, or that their own problems have harmed their son or daughter. When working with parents of disturbed or ill adolescents, it is very important to take such feelings into account.

Beyond this, the parents' mental health should be taken into account. Sometimes the parents' refusal to acknowledge the presence of disturbance or illness in their son or daughter contains the fear that they themselves are or may be mentally disturbed or ill. Such an assessment is important because it enables us to differentiate between the adolescent's own doubts or fears about help or treatment and the doubts or fears of the parents.

If treatment or help are seen from the adolescent's or his parents' points of view, often they have no idea what is or may be going wrong in the adolescent's life, what treatment involves, or how to judge whether one form of help is more suitable than another. Some adolescents or their parents seem ready to try anything, as long as it holds out some hope or promise for change. Most are unable to ask for information about the kind of help being offered, why it is being suggested in the first place, or who will be responsible for the treatment. More often, they simply feel grateful and relieved that something is being done, and are unable to make any enquiries which may imply that the professional person's judgement or authority is being questioned.

The most serious difficulty which adolescents and parents may face is that of wrong assessment, casual advice and incorrect understanding of the problem by the professional person to whom they have gone for help. This includes the doctor, the social worker, the counsellor, the tutor and the teacher. Nobody should automatically accept what they are told; mental disturbance, illness and breakdown in adolescence have too serious an effect on people's lives for these to be viewed casually or dismissed as not being of much concern. Nor should people who are worried be satisfied with vague promises or reassurances or with being sent from one person or clinic to the next without any help or treatment being given.

Forms of help or treatment

Most of the services which are available at present do not make special provision for adolescents, but in recent years various services — treatment centres, wards in hospitals, day-care hostels — have been set up specifically for adolescents, but these exist only in a few places in Britain.

Information about the psychological and social services which exist can usually be obtained by contacting the social services department, education department, or the health department in the borough.

Psychological assessment services

Psychological assessment can be obtained through the psychiatric service in a hospital, the child guidance clinics, or through some of the services which have been set up specifically for adolescents and young people. An appointment with the psychiatric service is usually made through one's family doctor. Alternatively, the child guidance clinic in the area can be contacted and help requested either through the clinic itself or through one of the services in the area. A problem often faced by adolescents and parents is that there are few psychological services for those who are beyond school-leaving age, but who are not yet considered to be 'adults'.

Advisory and counselling services

These services advise adolescents about work, school, the
services which exist in the community (employment, youth
clubs, social services), and about personal problems. The range
of help varies from one service to the next, and this may
depend on the staff. Some of these services have professionally
trained staff who are experienced in the assessment and
treatment of young people; others have mainly voluntary staff.

Psychological treatment

In general such treatment usually aims at bringing about a
change within the person himself; it is carried out mainly
through talking, where the professional person (psychiatrist,
psychoanalyst, psychotherapist, psychologist) tries to help the
patient understand what it is that has brought about his
problem. There are a number of important differences
between the various forms of psychological treatment. Those
patients who agree to undertake a specific form of treatment
should have clarified for them what the treatment is, what it
will aim to do, how long it will go on for and who will carry it
out.

    Of the various forms of psychological treatment described
below, those which are available on the National Health Service
or through some local authority services are individual psychotherapy
(usually a maximum of one appointment each week), group
psychotherapy, family therapy and psychotherapeutic
communities. Psychoanalytic treatment and individual
psychotherapy (of more than one appointment each week)
are, at present, available mainly through private treatment.

Psychoanalytic treatment. This aims at understanding those
factors, both historical and more recent, which have brought
about the disturbance or breakdown. The emphasis is not only
on experiences, events or feelings which the patient can remember,
but on those which may not be conscious and which still have
influence on his present behaviour and feelings.

    The psychoanalyst and the patient meet four or five times
each week for about an hour each time. Treatment takes place

through talking; the psychoanalyst helps the patient understand the history and meaning of his problems, and the motivation for his behaviour.

Individual psychotherapy. This treatment may aim at understanding the causes of the disturbance or at removing the symptoms — the aim may be determined by the severity of the disturbance or the intensity of the treatment. Individual psychotherapy may be based on psychoanalytic understanding of the mind or on various psychiatric views of mental disturbance or illness.

The psychotherapist and the patient may meet once, twice or three times each week for about one hour each time. Treatment takes place through talking; however, in those instances where the patient feels very anxious or depressed drugs may temporarily be prescribed in conjunction with the psychotherapy.

Group psychotherapy. A number of patients, usually six to eight, are treated together in a group by one psychotherapist. The discussion which takes place is intended to give the patients an understanding of their behaviour and the behaviour of the others in the group. The group usually meets for about an hour and a half, once or twice weekly.

Family therapy. This is based on the assumption that the problems for which one member of the family needs help are dependent on various factors within the family, and that the different members of the family may be in need of help or treatment. It is usual, therefore, for a number of members of the family to attend together for discussion and possibly for treatment.

Psychotherapeutic communities. These aim at having contact with larger groups of patients as, for example, in wards of hospitals. The patients and the staff of the ward may have meetings in which all patients in the group or in the ward are encouraged to talk about what they feel and think. The aim of the therapeutic community is

At this Centre adolescents can walk in and receive help
from qualified staff

different from the aims of individual treatment; in the therapeutic community a primary aim is to encourage better communication and mutual understanding among patients.

Another type of psychotherapeutic community is the day hospital. The patients usually live at home but come to the day hospital each day for activities, meetings, treatment and care. This form of care and treatment is used for those patients who need not be admitted to hospital, but who may nevertheless not be well enough to attend school or keep a job.

Hypnosis. The patient is in a trance-like state during the treatment session; during this time he is helped to release repressed emotions. Those people who practise hypnosis believe that the release of these repressed emotions will relieve the patient and may also remove the symptoms of the disturbance. When the patient comes out of this state, he does not remember what has taken place when he was in a trance.

Physical forms of treatment

Physical treatment aims at alleviating anxiety, tension or depression. It does not remove the causes of the problems for which the patient needs help; it is usually intended more to relieve the patient. If physical treatment is advised as an appropriate form of help, the adolescent and his parents should understand the aims of the treatment, why it is being suggested, and what other forms of treatment are available as alternatives.

Drug treatment. Tranquillizers are drugs which aim primarily at alleviating anxiety and tension. Various drugs are used for this purpose — these are prescribed by either a doctor or a psychiatrist. They are identified by their trade names; for example, largactil, stelazine, librium, valium. **Anti-depressants** are drugs prescribed mainly for purposes of relieving depression. Their trade names include tofranil, tryptizol, nardil, marplan, benzedrine, dexedrine.

There are various other drugs available, such as hallucinogenic drugs (lysergic acid diethylamid/LSD and mescaline), abreactive drugs (trade names such as pentathol, methedrine, sodium amytal), and sedatives. LSD and mescaline have been used in some research into mental illness; both LSD and mescaline can bring about temporary psychotic-like thoughts and behaviour. Abreactive drugs may produce unconsciousness, and this may be followed by a trance-like state; these drugs are sometimes used in conjunction with some psychological treatment. Opinions vary a good deal about the advantages and disadvantages of their uses in psychological treatment. Sedatives are used to allay anxiety or to promote undisturbed sleep; these are usually prescribed by a doctor.

Shock therapy. Electroconvulsion therapy (ECT) has been used most often with patients experiencing long-standing depression. Its way of acting on the patient is not well understood, and it is now used mainly if relief from severe depression is not brought about by anti-depressant drugs. An electric current is passed into the patient's body through electrodes which are placed on either side of the head. The electric current produces a convulsion. Recently, muscle relaxants have been administered to the patient as a preliminary so as to eliminate the danger of physical harm from the convulsion.

I have met a number of adolescents who have had this form of physical treatment. They have been frightened and bewildered by it, and were also temporarily unable to remember things. They were left with the feeling that they were irreparably harmed in some way. This is a form of physical treatment which seems most unsuitable for adolescents, no matter how disturbed or ill they are.

Insulin shock, until recently, was a therapy used in hospitals in the treatment of some mentally ill people, especially those diagnosed as suffering from schizophrenia. Its aim was to treat this illness, but we now know that this form of treatment temporarily removed some symptoms. Increased doses of insulin are administered to the patient over a period of days, until coma occurs. The coma is stopped by the administration of glucose.

Insulin shock therapy has now been replaced in most hospitals by drug therapy or ECT or both. Nevertheless, there

are still some hospitals which use this form of treatment.
Adolescents and parents should not agree to such treatment,
primarily because it does not seem to be of help, and also
because it can be frightening and dangerous.

Behaviour therapy

Behaviour therapy aims at alleviating or eliminating symptoms.
It attempts to alter the patient's behaviour in a specific
situation so that an undesirable reaction is replaced by a more
desirable one.

One form of such therapy is desensitization — this is a form
of deconditioning which aims at reducing phobias or fears by
accustoming the patient to those situations which ordinarily
bring about the fear. This form of treatment is used to
alleviate sexual fears which produce frigidity or impotence, to
control some forms of asthma, or to help the person control his
fear of people.

Another form of behaviour therapy is aversion. The
treatment aims at stopping the patient from behaving in
certain ways by linking that behaviour with something
unpleasant. Aversion therapy has been used with people who,
for instance, are homosexual, or alcoholic. In these instances,
the patient will, in treatment, experience something
unpleasant whenever he behaves in a way that he wants
to give up. He may, for example, be made to feel
nauseous when he drinks alcohol or when he comes into
contact with somebody of the same sex. Behavior therapy
is a relatively new procedure; its application to help or treat
mentally disturbed or ill adolescents is not well understood.

Psychosurgery

Brain surgery has been used for various mental illnesses. The
best known form of surgery is leucotomy (which means the
'cutting of white matter'). There have been many
modifications of this operation during the past thirty years or
so. It has been used to relieve symptoms such as severe depression,

chronic anxiety, compulsive behaviour, and acute emotional tension. It is not unusual for the patient to require some social support following this operation.

Although there is much controversy about the use of psychosurgery, it is still carried out in some hospitals. Once such an operation is carried out, the results of it cannot be reversed. It should never be accepted either by the adolescent or his parents as a way of treating mental disturbance or illness.

CHAPTER 6
THREE CASE HISTORIES

Alan

Alan, aged nineteen, came for help because he was worried about his attraction to other boys. This was affecting his work and he had left school early: 'I couldn't be bothered; it was a waste of time.'

He was fifteen when he first began to feel attracted to other boys. Although he was terrified of his homosexual feelings at the time, he nevertheless could not stop himself from thinking about certain boys. He spent all his free time in the school library because he felt that he could be near them more safely and inconspicuously there. There came a point when he began to be very frightened of his own feelings, fearing that he might lose control and actually try to touch a boy.

As a way of trying to control his feelings, he began to stay away from school. This finally resulted in his decision to leave school, which meant that it abruptly ended any possibility of going to university. His teachers were surprised at his decision, and his parents could not understand what had made him do this. He felt too ashamed to tell anybody of his feelings of attraction for boys. He took a job as a clerk, and he was in this job when he came for help.

Had Alan not been old enough to leave school he might have been classed as a 'school refuser'; that is, somebody refusing to attend school, but as he was nearly of school-leaving age he was not viewed as a case of 'school refusal'. So he did leave or, more correctly, he chose to remove himself from the field of danger, the school.

Soon after this, his disturbance took a more serious turn. Instead of simply feeling attracted to other boys he began to feel suspicious of men, and he developed the fear that they would attack him. In other words, the attraction to other boys and the feeling that he was bad and dirty developed into the idea that 'men may attack me' which contained the idea both of being touched and overpowered by men and also of being punished for these thoughts, which Alan considered to be dirty and shameful. Together with this, his own murderous fantasies were thought to exist in the minds of his fantasied attackers.

Of course, Alan had no conscious awareness of what was happening; he simply believed that what he was feeling was factually true. He felt so convinced of being attacked that he took to carrying a knife. He explained to me that he did not intend to harm anybody, but the knife was only 'to protect myself in case anybody has a go at me'. Temporarily, Alan was reacting in a way which showed signs of mental illness; in other words he could not differentiate between what was being created by his mind and what was in fact happening outside himself.

He was arrested by the police for carrying an offensive weapon. When he told them that he had recently sought help for his worries, they contacted me to confirm this. I explained that Alan was behaving in a way that indicated mental illness, and though the police were very worried that he might harm somebody, they decided not to charge him. It was, instead, decided to go ahead with arrangements to make treatment available for Alan; clearly he needed this urgently. It was possible also to arrange for Alan to go into hospital temporarily until his fear of being attacked or, more accurately, until his homosexual panic had subsided. The admission to hospital was necessary because of Alan's illness at that point. He needed care, and also I felt that treatment should not begin until Alan was in an environment where he could be protected and temporarily looked after. The hospital agreed that he could attend his treatment appointments outside the hospital.

Alan was already vulnerable before he reached adolescence. He was described as a shy child, with few friends, taken up with his own fantasy world and, as we might expect, he was 'no trouble'. When he reached sexual maturity, his fight against his homosexual wishes and fears began to collapse; before adolescence this fight was of a different nature — he withdrew, and spent most of his time in the presence of his parents completely taken up with his hobby of stamp-collecting. His difficulties went unnoticed.

The sad thing is that Alan was already nineteen by the time he sought help. By that time a great deal of damage had already taken place, some of which might have been prevented had he been spotted and helped four or five years earlier. At this point, Alan conveyed a picture of the presence of serious disturbance which developed to 'breakdown'. Although his sense of reality was impaired, this was linked to his 'homosexual panic', and during treatment it became clear that the impairment, although serious, was not permanent.

In addition to being temporarily in hospital where he could be cared for, I saw Alan for psychotherapy three times each week, and each interview lasted one hour. In treatment, Alan talked of his fear, dating back to when he was seven, that he might change into a girl. He had always felt that his body was too small. His father, whom Alan described as a bully, always made him feel small and a failure and he felt convinced that his father never cared for him much. When I met Alan's father, he turned out to be very different from the way in which Alan had described him. He was a gentle man, very worried about his son, and he felt very guilty about Alan's present serious disturbance. He had been concerned about his son for a long time, but had hesitated to seek any help for Alan because he thought that his trouble might be 'inherited'. The father referred to his own brother who had been in a mental hospital some years ago, and he worried that 'trouble may run in the family'; something which in fact had nothing to do with Alan's present disturbance.

Alan used to like being on his own. He would imagine boys being nice to him, and he liked feeling that he was being cared for by them. He was never able to be angry with either of his parents, especially his father; that is often a danger sign. He always did what he was told, and if he felt angry he would 'keep it in myself, then it would just disappear'. The image of himself which he now had was of being a child who was cared for by older men, as if he was a girl being protected by them; but the homosexual thoughts also included anger with these men and his wish to attack them in some way. Instead of attacking them, he saw in them what he himself was feeling, and he then felt frightened that he would be attacked.

It took a period of treatment before Alan could begin to recognize that his fear of being attacked was his way of expressing his own wish to attack, as well as his wish to be overpowered by a man. Before adolescence, this picture of himself as a shy, small boy did not produce too much danger because he could protect himself by staying home and remaining isolated. When he reached sexual maturity this wish and fear of having contact with boys or men took on the additional dimension of sexual contact with them. It was this wish and fear which made Alan progressively more unable to cope, resulting finally in his breakdown.

During the period in treatment when he felt overwhelmed by his thoughts and fears, he found it impossible to work or to be near people. Treatment enabled him to see that his thoughts of being attacked were created by his own mind, and that this danger did not actually exist. Alan remains a vulnerable young man, and is still frightened that he might again be overwhelmed by his thoughts. His treatment has continued for eighteen months, and he is now able to spend some time with boys of his own age. Recently he has thought of asking a girl to go out with him, but he has not yet been able to do this; he still thinks that people know he is 'odd'. It will require a further period of treatment before Alan will find it possible to function more normally at work and with his peers.

Alan was not really homosexual at all. His was more of a homosexual panic. The question of homosexuality or heterosexuality in his case was only a small part of the whole picture; his problem was more related to his distorted view of the outside world, to his fear of people, to his belief that he was abnormal, and to his belief that he was prone to being attacked.

Rebecca

Rebecca, aged sixteen, came to see me at the suggestion of her teacher, who had spoken to me. 'What worries me about her is that she does all right one day but she's impossible the next. I also feel that her staying away for one or two days at a time isn't good. She doesn't talk much about herself. I feel that she is a girl who has everything to live for but she conveys the feeling that she wouldn't mind if she were dead.'

In the initial interviews I had with Rebecca it became clear to me that she was a very depressed person who was constantly taken up with her own badness and with thoughts about dying. When, with Rebecca's agreement, I talked with her parents, they too conveyed great concern about her, but said 'We didn't know what to do about it, so we thought we would let it go for a while. We asked her a number of times why she felt depressed, but she would answer that she didn't know and that some of her friends felt the same way about life.'

Rebecca was very hesitant at first to describe what she felt 'because it all sounds so silly when I put it into words; it's as if it doesn't sound like anything'. She felt that her attitude to life changed suddenly at about the age of thirteen or fourteen. She used to think of herself as happy, but suddenly it was as if she couldn't be bothered to get out of bed in the morning. She remembered that soon after she began to menstruate at the age of thirteen, she used to feel as if she had 'a load of muck' inside her, as if she hated her body for producing the pain and the 'dirty blood'. 'I know it's silly, but sometimes I can't get away from thinking these things.' She began to feel that she was overweight, not as pretty as her friends, and that nobody would ever really like her. She knew that what she felt was unrealistic, but at the same time she felt that she could not stop these thoughts about herself.

At fifteen she had intercourse with her boyfriend. This, too, was a disappointment because it did not remove the feeling that there was something wrong with her, that is, that she might not be normal in some way. She said, 'After I had intercourse, I felt as if there was nothing else to live for. I had just about tried everything, and I still felt empty. So I didn't know what to do next.'

She stayed away from school one or two days each month during her menstrual periods, because it was especially during that time that she could not be bothered to get out of bed, and 'that's the time I would hate myself most. I would cry without knowing why'. Although many girls normally feel depressed and are preoccupied with their bodies during their menstrual periods, I felt that Rebecca was describing reactions which went beyond the normal, that is, she was describing herself as a person who felt empty and bad and did not really want to live. Her view of the future was described as 'it feels as if it doesn't matter, as if I don't care whether it will be good or bad, but somehow, I feel it won't be good'.

When I talked to her parents, her mother described Rebecca as having been quite a lively child, but as somebody who would suddenly look sad. Rebecca would at times be playing with her friends and would suddenly burst into tears. She remembered, too, that Rebecca would always have to come home as soon as school ended each day. Her mother had been ill with pneumonia when Rebecca was eight, and during this time Rebecca found it almost impossible to leave her. This concern about her mother's health became a preoccupation, with Rebecca always asking her mother how she felt. The mother then described her own feeling of depression which lasted more or less from the time Rebecca was two until quite recently. Both parents were now concerned about their daughter because, as the mother said, 'I don't want her to go through the kinds of depressions I have gone through.

Although I was concerned about Rebecca and her present depression, I did not feel that she was at risk; there was no likelihood of a suicide attempt or of a 'breakdown'. The manner in which Rebecca described her depression, and the extent of her self-observation as well as her readiness to talk about her feelings made me feel that a period of psychotherapy could help her gain insight and understanding into the meaning of her present depression. The treatment consisted of one-hour interviews each week extending over a period of one year, though it would have been preferable to see Rebecca more often.

Rebecca was able to be helped to some extent by the psychotherapy. One important factor which contributed to her depression was her feeling, as a child, that she had to take care of her mother who was always so sad; it was as if Rebecca temporarily had to 'mother' her mother. At the same time, Rebecca grew up with the feeling that she must never be angry with her mother for fear that this anger would in some way harm her. It was as if she always had to be good, no matter what she felt. She was also very frightened as a child that her mother might die, and when she had pneumonia, Rebecca felt convinced that it was her fault. It was as if Rebecca's badness had made her mother ill. When, in adolescence, Rebecca had intercourse with her boyfriend, she felt convinced that if her mother found out 'it would kill her'. She was sure she had done a terrible thing, and when she then felt empty and dirty she believed that she deserved to feel this way.

By the time treatment ended, I felt that she was still prone to depression, but we had been able to understand some of its history. To some extent, the treatment also helped her cope with a crisis. She was able to stay on at school and to work for her A-levels instead of giving in to her depression, but I felt, also, that she would need further help later on. I discussed this with her and with her parents, and it was decided that Rebecca and I would keep in touch to see whether the depression still interfered in her daily life.

Bill

Bill, aged seventeen, sought help at the suggestion of his family doctor. He had recently been discharged from hospital after having made a serious suicide attempt. The doctor had hoped that Bill would be kept in hospital for a period when he might be offered psychiatric treatment, but instead he was discharged three days after having been admitted. He had taken seventy aspirins, and was found in bed semi-conscious by his father. Bill's parents were quite ready to take the advice of friends to 'forget about it — quite a few adolescents do things like that', but the family doctor insisted that something must be done to help him, feeling that without treatment Bill was at risk of killing himself. I agreed with the doctor.

My experience has shown repeatedly that any adolescent who attempts suicide is not only at risk now, but also in the future, and that every adolescent whom I have seen who had attempted suicide is urgently in need of care and treatment. do not believe that an action which endangers a person's life can be viewed simply as a wish for attention or as a wish to shock people. I always view attempted suicide in adolescence as a sign of breakdown.

When Bill first came to discuss the possibility of treatment, he said he felt unsure about the need for it. He came only because his doctor had insisted that he seek help. Bill's parents, too, were unsure about the logic of his need for treatment, saying that he seemed much better now and that the 'cause' of the suicide attempt had now been dealt with. They were referring to the fact that Bill and his girlfriend had now 'made it up again'. As described in Chapter 4 many people believe that an event such as a boy- or girlfriend leaving, or failing an exam, or having an argument with a parent, or losing a job, causes a person to attempt suicide. This is never the explanation. Instead, it is the case that an event confirms for the adolescent his own longstanding feeling of worthlessness or abnormality, and to him the suicide attempt is a way of attacking his own body and doing away with it by killing it. Every suicide attempt also contains an attack on a person other than oneself, but by this time the person being attacked is in the mind of the one who is attempting the suicide. From the point of view of assessment, I believe that every suicide attempt must be viewed as an episode where the sense of reality has temporarily been lost. I also think that those people who attempt suicide are likely to attempt it again unless they receive psychological treatment for breakdown.

I told Bill what I thought, but he at first rejected this, repeating that everything was all right now. He and his parents were unsure what decision to take about treatment, so we arranged to meet again. In fact, Bill and I met four times to discuss all his doubts and fears about treatment, as well as to discuss his idea that treatment might make him 'mad'. I had suggested to Bill that the treatment to choose should be daily one-hour appointments for psychoanalysis, that is, five times each week. At first, Bill felt convinced that this suggestion of mine reflected my belief that he was crazy. In fact, it reflected my belief that Bill was now very vulnerable and that the treatment had to aim at removing the cause of his breakdown, rather than supporting him or helping him over the present crisis. Bill finally agreed to this treatment.

Until the time of his suicide attempt, Bill thought of himself as a shy, introspective, person who was 'happy enough'. But, as he recalled the earlier period of his adolescence and some of his childhood, he remembered a great deal which he had 'simply forgotten' but which described a very unhappy, isolated, and good person who always had to be outstanding in his studies. He was considered by his teachers to be a brilliant student, and he was planning to go to university outside London. However, because of his suicide attempt and of the continued risk which existed, I advised him to go to a university in London so that he could continue with treatment.

He remembered one event in his childhood which he felt was devastating for him. He had a pet cat from the age of seven to nine. One day it disappeared and he never saw it again. He mourned for the cat for many months; he felt that his badness may have contributed to the cat's disappearance and that, in any case, it most probably did not like him. He searched for it each day for months but he never found it. He then felt that it might be preferable not to have a pet because 'one becomes fond of it and it then leaves'. 'It was my best friend, and after that I never really had a best friend. My brother was never a friend in the same way as my cat.'

At puberty, he responded to his physically mature body by denying the changes which were taking place. He never touched his penis because, as he said, 'That's dirty and makes you bad.' Once when he had a nocturnal emission he thought it would be better if he did not have a penis; but he then forgot about this thought, and simply felt that his physically mature body was always making demands on him which he thought were wrong. When he first met the girl who was later to become his girlfriend, he felt that his relationship with her would be 'sublime', which for Bill meant that sexual feelings would not spoil it. During the time that they went out together, Bill avoided any physical contact with her. Once, when she asked Bill what was wrong, he assumed that she meant to say 'What is wrong with you; are you abnormal in some way?' When she then said that she did not want to see him any longer 'because I want to go out with other boys as well', he took this as a confirmation of his abnormality. It was then that he took the seventy aspirins.

Although the suicide attempt seemed to be a sudden decision, Bill had been thinking of it for some time. He had thought that 'one day I might want to do something'. He had put away the aspirins 'just in case', even though he had no specific plan to use them.

There have been a number of crises during the period of treatment. At one point Bill had to be re-admitted to hospital because I thought there was the danger of another suicide attempt. He stayed in hospital just over one month, and during this time he continued to come for treatment. On two occasions, when he began to feel much better, he said that he had decided to stop coming. I was aware, from the treatment of other adolescents who are at risk, that 'feeling much better' is in no way a sign that treatment should end, but that it is a time when the adolescent must be protected from his own unreal belief that everything is fine. 'Feeling better' or 'everything is fine' may, in the case of the adolescent who has attempted suicide, have to be taken as a signal that a feeling of worthlessness or a wish to die will reappear very soon. In Bill's case, feeling better meant partly that he now felt less alone with his thoughts, that he began to believe that I would be able to help him, and that he began to find himself more able to trust me. But this did not mean that we had as yet understood what had brought about his feeling of worthlessness and his wish to kill himself. If treatment had ended when Bill thought it should, he would have remained seriously at risk and in danger of killing himself.

Bill's treatment has continued for the past two years. There have been a number of important changes in his life: he is less worried that the feelings coming from his body will make him 'mad'; he is now more aware that his wish to die represented a wish to do away with his feelings of being worthless and abnormal; he is now aware that his suicide attempt was meant to hurt and sadden his parents, and he has understood that it contained his despair, his self-hatred and his belief that nothing could ever change in his life. He remains vulnerable to feeling useless and bad, and it will still require a period of treatment to understand the history of the development of these feelings. Unless this is understood, the vulnerability to another suicide attempt or to other self-desctructive behaviour will remain.

Further reading

A. Aichhorn, **Wayward Youth,** Imago Publishing, (1925), 1951.
A description of work with disturbed delinquent adolescents. A
fascinating story of the lives of some of these adolescents, and how they
were able to be helped.

P. Blos, **On Adolescence,** Free Press, 1962.
A detailed discussion of normal development in adolescence, using
psychoanalytic concepts. A number of case histories included.

E. H. Erikson, **Childhood and Society,** Penguin, (1950), 1965.
A description of the development of conflicts of children in a number
of different cultures, with many detailed descriptions of their behaviour,
their family relationships and family expectations.

A. Freud, 'Adolescence', **Psychoanalytic Study of the Child,** vol. 13,
International Universities Press, 1960.
A psychoanalytic description of the normal problems facing adolescents
in their emotional development to adulthood.

A. Freud, **Normality and Pathology in Childhood,** International
Universities Press, 1965; Penguin, 1973.
A comprehensive description of the psychoanalytic principles of
development as applied to children, including descriptions of childhood
disturbances and of problems in treatment.

S. Freud, **Three Essays on the Theory of Sexuality,** Hogarth Press,
(1905), 1953.
This is the first mention by Freud of the problems encountered in
normal development during adolescence. In this paper, Freud defines
the areas which produce stress.

S. Freud, **New Introductory Lectures on Psychoanalysis,** Hogarth Press,
(1933), 1964.
A comprehensive outline of the principles of psychoanalysis, including
that of development and treatment.

M. Mead, **From the South Seas: Studies of Adolescence and Sex in
Primitive Societies,** Morrow, 1939.
A detailed description, by a famous social anthropologist, of the life
and expectations of young people in primitive societies.

F. Musgrove, **Youth and the Social Order,** Routledge & Kegan Paul, 1964.
A very interesting description of adolescents, and the attitudes of people to adolescents, over the years. Describes changes in social organization, laws, attitudes.

T. Parker, **Five Women,** Hutchinson, 1965.
Detailed descriptions, in personal terms, of five women in prison. Descriptions of their families, their lives and their present views.

E. Stengel, **Suicide and Attempted Suicide,** Penguin, 1964.

J. M. Tanner, **Growth at Adolescence,** Blackwell, 1962.
A very comprehensive description of physical development in adolescence. Many examples of the normal expectation of physical development.

D. W. Winnicott, **The Child, The Family and the Outside World,** Penguin, 1964.
A number of papers describing the child's development, the relationship between the child and the family organization, the problems encountered during development, the role of the mother. A very helpful description of a number of important areas in the child's life, especially that of the child—mother relationship.

Index